DOGS

FACTS, FIGURES & FUN

"Any book without a mistake in it has had too much money spent on it"

Sir William Collins, publisher

DOGS

Facts, Figures & Fun

Iain Zaczek

ff&f

Dogs
Facts, Figures & Fun

Published by
Facts, Figures & Fun, an imprint of
AAPPL Artists' and Photographers' Press Ltd.
Church Farm House, Wisley, Surrey GU23 6QL
info@ffnf.co.uk www.ffnf.co.uk
info@aappl.com www.aappl.com

Sales and Distribution
UK and export: Turnaround Publisher Services Ltd.
orders@turnaround-uk.com
USA and Canada: Sterling Publishing Inc. sales@sterlingpub.com
Australia & New Zealand: Peribo Pty. peribomec@bigpond.com
South Africa: Trinity Books. trinity@iafrica.com

A catalogue record for this book is available from the
British Library.

ISBN 13: 9781904332503
ISBN 10: 1904332501

Design (contents and cover): Malcolm Couch
mal.couch@blueyonder.co.uk

Printed in China by Imago Publishing
info@imago.co.uk

CONTENTS

INTRODUCTION

No one can be certain exactly when or how dogs evolved, but they were undoubtedly in existence by around 10,000 BC. Some of the earliest evidence comes from cave paintings, which show humans and dog-like creatures hunting alongside each other. Then, as now, the two species formed a unique partnership.

In zoological terms, dogs belong to the *canidae* family. In addition to the dog (*canis*), this includes the wolf (*canis lupus*), the fox (*canis vulpes*), the jackal (*canis aureus*), and various types of wild dog. The precise relationship between these animals has been the subject of much debate, but dogs' closest links are undoubtedly with wolves. There are notable similarities between their teeth and their skull formation, and both animals share a pack mentality. Many naturalists believe that the dog is descended directly from the wolf.

The earliest ancestor of the dog is much disputed. The *myocis*, the *daphocnodon*, and the *cynodictis* have all been suggested by palaeontologists. The first domesticated dog was given the name *canis familiaris palustris* (the Marsh or

Peat Dog) by the Swiss naturalist, Ludwig Rutimeyer (1825-95). The teeth-marks left on gnawed bones show that this animal was sharing human food from a very early stage.

The sheer diversity of modern breeds has raised the question of common ancestry. Can a Chihuahua really come from the same source as a St. Bernard? Opinion is divided, although mutations and selective breeding can account for many of the changes. Dogs also had to adapt to very different climates and environments. A thick coat was obviously vital for survival in Arctic conditions, but a liability in tropical temperatures. Disease may also have played a part. Some naturalists believe that the ancestors of the short-nosed breeds were affected by *achondroplasia* – a congenital affliction that can stunt the growth of certain bones.

The process of diversification was already well advanced, prior to the appearance of written records. From their artworks, for example, it is clear that the ancient Egyptians kept more than a dozen breeds of dog, ranging from Mastiffs, Greyhounds, and Deerhounds to smaller dogs that resembled modern-day Basset Hounds and Dachshunds.

With their passion for hunting, the Greeks soon added to this number. They also produced some of the earliest literature on the subject. Dogs appear frequently in the stories of Homer (8th c. BC) and the histories of Thucydides (born c.500 BC), while Xenophon's (c.428-

c.354 BC) *Cynegeticus* ('Hunting') was the first treatise to contain detailed information on dogs. Among other things, it discussed their origins, their breeding potential, and their usage in different types of hunt.

Studies of this kind multiplied during the Roman era. In his book on the subject, Gratius Faliscus listed no fewer than 22 different types of hound, from all parts of the empire. Roman authors also provided information on the treatment of canine diseases, kennel management and farm dogs. From more general sources, there are also indications that pet ownership was on the rise, and that these lapdogs were highly pampered. One wit enquired if the ladies of Rome had forsaken the practice of having babies, in favour of having dogs. Similarly, in one of his *Epigrams*, Martial (c.AD 40-103/4) satirised a friend's slavish devotion to his dog: 'Issa is purer than the kiss of a dove. Issa is more tender than all the young maidens. Issa is more precious than the sapphires of India. When she gives a tiny whine, you would have thought she spoke...'

Even in areas that did not produce records of this kind, it is clear that dogs were flourishing. Many classical authors wrote admiringly of the animals that were available in Gaul and Britain. Strabo (64 BC-c. AD 24), for example, commented that 'there is a certain strong breed of hunting dogs, small, but worthy of sublime praise, which the wild tribes of Britain maintain'.

The earliest attempts to catalogue the various dog breeds in English did not occur until the Middle Ages. Here, the

The Classification of Dogs, according to Linnaeus.

Since the 18th century, many of these terms
have been changed.

Canis familiaris	Faithful Dog
Canis aquaticus minor	Lesser Water Dog
Canis domesticus	Shepherd's Dog
Canis pomeranus	Pomeranian
Canis sibericus	Siberian Dog
Canis parvus melitans	Little Maltese Dog
Canis islandicus	Iceland Dog
Canis aquaticus major	Great Water Dog (Grand Barbet)
Canis hibernicus	Irish Dog
Canis turcicus	Turkish Hound
Canis pilosus	Hairy Maltese Dog
Canis leoninus	Lion Dog
Canis variegatus	Little Danish Dog
Canis graius	Scotch Hunting Dog
Canis fricator	Pug Dog
Canis graius hirsutus	Rough Scotch Hunting Dog
Canis molossus	Bulldog
Canis italicus	Italian Greyhound
Canis orientalis	Persian Greyhound

Canis egyptius	Hairless Greyhound
Canis sagax	German Hound
Canis laniaris	Lurcher
Canis fuillus	Boarhound
Canis anglicus or	Mastiff
Canis bellicosus	
Canis gallicus	Hound
Canis vertigus	Turnspit
Canis scoticus	Bloodhound
Canis americanus	Ala
Canis avicularis	Pointer
Canis antarcticus	New Holland Dog
Canis aquatilis	Barbet
Canis cursorius	Greyhound
Canis hybridus	Bastard Pug Dog
Canis extratius or	Spaniel also called
Canis hyspanicus	Rocquet

pioneering text was the *Boke of St. Albans* (1486), written by Dame Juliana Berners. This dealt principally with hunting dogs, but it was very popular and was reprinted many times. It was eventually superseded by the more general classification, which was compiled by Dr. Johannes Caius in 1570. On the continent, the most influential book on hunting was produced by Gaston de Foix (1331-91). Its meticulous illustrations have proved particularly valuable for historians, revealing the precise appearance of some of the early, vanished breeds. In later years, groundbreaking catalogues were also assembled by the naturalists Carl Linnaeus (1707-78) and Buffon (1707-88).

Even today, not all dogs are domesticated. Several feral breeds are still in existence in various parts of the world. Unlike ordinary strays, these wild dogs can form viable communities – forming into packs and breeding success-fully. The main variety is the Dingo, which is sometimes also known as the Australian Native Dog or the Warrigal. This is a very ancient dog – the earliest remains date back to 1450 BC. More importantly, it is also one of the purest breeds, for the simple reason that its isolation in the Australian outback prevented much cross-breeding. Nevertheless, the Dingo is also a considerable menace to livestock and is currently classed as vermin.

In contrast to the Dingo, the appearance of another feral breed – the Pariah or Pye Dog – varies considerably from place to place. As the name suggests, the Pariah is an outcast and has flourished most in those areas, where there has been cultural opposition to the practice of dog ownership. In a number of Hindu, Jewish and Moslem texts, they are defined as unclean animals, and the word 'dog' is sometimes used as a term of abuse. Pariah dogs are most common in southern Asia and certain parts of the Middle East.

In the past, dogs were kept mainly as working animals or hunters. Today, the vast majority are pets, valued more for their companionship than any practical purpose. Even the most pampered pet, however, still displays some vestiges of the natural instincts, passed down from its ancient, feral state. When a dog runs after a ball or a stick, for instance, it is responding to a basic hunting instinct – to chase after a fast-moving object. Dogs are still highly territorial. The male dog marks out its territory by urinating at strategic points. Some dogs may guard their territory by attacking any material that comes through the letter-box. Postmen may arouse particular ire, because they persist in breaching territorial boundaries, even though they have been repeatedly warned off. Within the home, dogs still retain a primitive, pack mentality, accepting the family unit as a variation of this grouping. As long as they are well trained, they will happily defer to the food-provider as the leader of the pack. If their training is neglected, they may assume a more dominant role, resulting in bad behaviour. When a dog barks, it is an alarm call, urging other members of the pack/family to come quickly. Dogs can exist quite contentedly in a pack that has just two members – themselves and their owner – but they hate to be left alone. When this occurs, they may howl dolefully, pleading with other members of the pack to come and join them.

Worldwide, the number of households with pet dogs
continues to rise, passing the 200 million mark in the
1990s. A survey in 1993 listed the leading dog-owning
areas as follows:

North America	60 million
France	10.8 million
Russia	10 million
UK	7.2 million
Japan	7 million
Italy	5 million
Germany	4.5 million
Australia	3.1 million
Spain	2.9 million
Scandinavia	2 million
Belgium	1.6 million
Netherlands	1.4 million

CANINE QUOTATIONS

The reason a dog has so many friends is that he wags his tail instead of his tongue.
Anonymous

Don't accept your dog's admiration as conclusive evidence that you are wonderful.
Ann Landers

If there are no dogs in Heaven, then when I die I want to go where they went.
Will Rogers

A dog is the only thing on earth that loves you more than he loves himself.
Josh Billings

The average dog is a nicer person than the average person.
Andy Rooney

We give dogs time we can spare, space we can spare and love we can spare.
And in return, dogs give us their all.
It's the best deal man has ever made.
M. Acklam

Dogs love their friends and bite their enemies, quite unlike people, who are incapable of pure love and always have to mix love and hate.
Sigmund Freud

RELIGION, MYTHOLOGY & SUPERSTITION

Given the close nature of the partnership between humans and their favourite animal, it is hardly surprising that dogs became associated with the religious beliefs and the folklore of many cultures. In ancient Egypt, there were strong canine links with the god Anubis. Although usually described as a jackal, visual depictions of the deity were often based on the Pariah or Pye dog. Anubis performed several functions relating to death and the afterlife. He was the god of embalming rites and the protector of cemeteries. He also judged the souls of the dead, by weighing their hearts on the Scales of Truth. During the Graeco-Roman period of Egyptian history, the god became associated with Hermes, and was often called Hermanubis. In the visual arts, the deity was either portrayed as a straightforward jackal, or as a man with a dog or jackal's head.

Quite apart from their links with Anubis, dogs also played an important part in Egypt's elaborate cult of death. When the Greek historian, Herodotus (c.490–c.425 BC), visited the country, he was surprised to find that house-holds went into deep mourning when their dogs died and that their mummified remains were buried in special graveyards. In the same way, they were sometimes placed in the tombs of the pharaohs, in wooden, dog-shaped coffins. The widespread practice of mummifying dogs has aroused the interest of today's historians, who hope to find sufficient traces of DNA, to reveal new information about the development of certain, ancient breeds.

The Pekingese used to have powerful spiritual associa-tions in China. When the country adopted Buddhism as its religion, it automatically accepted the Buddhist lion as one of its holy symbols. Lions were not native to China, however, so local artists were often unsure how to portray them. Then, noticing a superficial resemblance between their own Pekingese dog and foreign depictions of lions, they produced an amalgam of the two – the Lion-Dog. After this, statues of Lion-Dogs would often be placed as guardians, at the entrances of temples and imperial palaces.

Pekes were strongly associated with the Court. They enjoyed a luxurious existence, raised by eunuchs and included in many imperial ceremonies. At royal funerals, they were led before the coffin of the deceased. The sale or removal of these dogs from the Court precincts was strictly forbidden, and the breed was unknown in the West until 1860, when Peking was stormed by allied troops. One of the surviving dogs was presented to Queen Victoria.

The Peke was not the only dog to have religious connotations in the Orient. The Lhasa Apso was also held in great veneration. It served principally as a monastery dog, although it was always more than a mere companion. The dogs were widely regarded as symbols of good fortune, as well as instruments of reincarnation. If a monk died but failed to reach Nirvana, it was thought that he might be reborn as a monastery dog. Conversely, when an Apso died, some believed that he might be reincarnated as a human child.

Beyond this, there was an ancient legend linking the Lhasa Apso with the goddess Sako. This winged animal-deity dwelt in the mountains of Tibet, where she had two offspring. One of these could fly, while the other was flightless. The latter was identified as the first Apso. Like the Pekingese, Apsos were closely guarded from outside influences and were rarely seen in the West until the 20th century.

'I wonder if other dogs think poodles are members
of a weird religious cult.'
Rita Rudner

In Greek mythology the most famous dog was Cerberus, the triple-headed monster that guarded the gates of Hades. He had a barbed, serpent-like tail and, when a drop of his toxic saliva fell to the earth, it produced the poisonous plant, aconite. In the last and most difficult of his labours, Hercules was charged with the task of captur-

In Chinese astrology, 2006 is the year of the Dog. There are 12 animal signs in the cycle, so the previous year of the Dog was 1994. As in Western astrology, people with the same birth-sign are thought to share certain characteristics. Individuals born in a Dog year are said to be reliable, compassionate and honest, though they may also be anxious and pessimistic. These qualities are tempered by a second cycle, governed by the five Chinese elements – Metal, Wood, Fire, Earth, and Water. Accordingly, 2006 is the year of the Fire Dog. People born in this year will be natural leaders, full of drive and adventure. The last Fire Dog year was 1946. In terms of romance, Dogs are best suited to Tigers, Rabbits, Pigs, or other Dogs.

Celebrities born in the Year of the Dog

Andre Agassi
David Bowie
George W. Bush
Winston Churchill
Bill Clinton
Michael Jackson
Christopher Lee

Madonna
Mother Teresa
Elvis Presley
Steven Spielberg
Sylvester Stallone
Uma Thurman

ing this fearsome creature. The appearance of Cerberus was probably influenced by more ancient deities. There are links with the Egyptian jackal-god Anubis, who also dwelt in the underworld, and with the triple form of Hecate, the goddess of death.

In ancient Greece, there was an intriguing canine link with a well known philosophical sect. The Cynics took their name from *kynikos* ('dog-like'). This stemmed from their leader Diogenes (c.400–325 BC), who was nick-named 'the dog'. The association came about because, in his teachings, Diogenes urged his followers to discard any sense of shame – a notion that, in the eyes of some of his contemporaries, made him no better than a dog.

The Dog Star also took its name from Greek mythology, where Sirius was a two-headed hound belonging to Orion the hunter. The twin heads were symbolic, look-ing back to the Old Year and forward to the New Year. This also relates to the calendar adopted by the ancient Egyptians. They measured time in 'canicular' years, so-called because the start of the year was marked by the Dog-Star rising with the sun.

The Romans described the height of their summer as 'dog days' (*dies caniculares*, July 3 – August 11), because it coincided with the rising of Sirius, the Dog-Star. The term became proverbial for periods of intense heat, that were thought to drive dogs mad. Hence the line in the Noel Coward song, stating that only 'mad dogs and Englishmen go out in the midday sun'. The wild rose or 'dog-rose' gained its nickname, because the ancient Greeks believed that it could cure a mad dog's bite.

Dogs are rarely mentioned in the Bible and, even then, the tone is usually disparaging. Among other things, they are likened to enemies, false teachers, and impenitent sinners. In spite of this, there are several light-hearted, canine legends involving Noah's Ark. The most common of these suggests that the animal acquired its cold nose, when the vessel sprang a leak and a courageous dog plugged it with his snout. In a less heroic variation of this theme, the dog was simply the last creature to go aboard and, as there was no more room, he was left with part of his head poking out of the door. After being exposed to the elements in this way for 40 days, his nose was left with a permanent chill.

Only one breed of dog is mentioned by name in the Bible. This can be found in Proverbs XXX, 29-31: 'There are three things which go well, yea:... A lion, which is strongest among beasts, and turneth not away for any; A greyhound; An he-goat also...'

From ancient times, a dog's saliva was thought to have health-giving properties. In Christian lore, for example, St. Roch – the protector of plague victims – is closely associated with a dog. The latter is said to have nursed him back to health, when he was stricken with the illness. To illustrate this, images of the holy man frequently showed the dog licking a plague-sore on his master's thigh.

Saliva is not the only canine substance that has aroused the interest of the medical world. Dogs' milk, officially described as *Lac Caninum*, has been known for its curative powers since antiquity. The Greek physician Dioscorides (1st century AD) and the Roman author Pliny the Elder (AD 23/4–79) both recommended it as an antidote for poison and for treating a variety of other ailments. In modern times, interest in the substance was revived in the US. It is now regarded as a standard home-opathic remedy.

In the West, St. Christopher is mainly known as the patron saint of travellers and, when depicted by artists, he is usually shown carrying the Christ-child on his shoulders. In the East, however, he was sometimes portrayed on religious icons as a man with a dog's head. This Greek Orthodox version was influenced by an early account of the saint's martyrdom, which specified that Christopher belonged to the Marmaritae, an African tribe. When interrogated by his persecutors, he mentioned that 'my face shows you that I am of the race of the dog-heads'. Some artists interpreted this literally, but the comment was meant in a figurative sense. Prior to the age of discovery, there was a superstitious belief that strange creatures dwelt at the edges of the known world, among them a race of dog-headed people. Christopher's answer simply meant that he came from a very distant tribe. In the West, the text was translated differently. Early versions described the saint as *canineus* ('dog-like'), but this was soon changed to *cananeus* ('Canaanite'). Significantly, in Catholic lore, Christopher was defined as a Canaanite, rather than an African.

No dog has been named after Roch or Christopher, but two other saints have enjoyed this honour. Everyone has heard of the St. Bernard breed, which does not take its name from Bernard of Clairvaux (1090-1153), the champion of the Cistercian order of monks, but from the lesser known Bernard of Menthon (c.923-1008). In c.962, he set up a hospice in the Swiss Alps, offering aid and shelter to passing travellers. Dogs were introduced in the 17th century and soon proved their worth, by locating and rescuing victims, who had become trapped or buried in the snow.

St. Bernards are descended from Mastiffs and indeed, until the late 19th century, they were generally known as Alpine Mastiffs. In the 1830s, the monks produced a thick-coated variety of the breed, through a series of experimental crosses with Newfoundlands. Their aim was to produce a hardier dog, better suited to the harsh conditions, but the idea backfired, as the heavier coats simply became encrusted with ice. The breed almost became known as the Barry Dog, as a tribute to the most famous of the rescue dogs. Barry (1800-14) saved more than 40 lives and was fêted in a Disney film. His body is preserved at the Natural History Museum in Bern.

Sadly, the popular image of a St. Bernard carrying a cask of brandy around his neck is nothing more than a colourful invention. It stemmed from a painting by Sir Edwin Landseer (c.1802-73), which became so famous that the idea passed into canine folklore. As a result, the monks decided to keep a few casks at the hospice, so that visiting tourists would not be disappointed.

In its time, the dog named after St. Hubert (d.727) was even more famous. The St. Hubert's Hound is widely regarded as the prototype for most European scent-hounds, the ancestor of such breeds as the Bloodhound and the Basset Hound. The breed was so prestigious that the dogs were often used as royal gifts. Hubert's monastery presented six of the hounds each year to the French king.

From his youth, Hubert was passionate about hunting. According to legend, his conversion occurred when he was out hunting in a wood on Good Friday. In a clearing, he came upon a white stag with a crucifix lodged in its antlers. The vision prompted the young man to change his worldly ways, though he did not give up his sport. He developed his breed of hound while serving as the Bishop of Liège and, after his death, became known as the patron saint of hunting.

Dogs featured prominently in medieval bestiaries – books containing accounts of real and imaginary animals, that were mainly used to illustrate moral lessons. In these texts, they usually symbolised either fidelity or watchfulness. The link with faithfulness had been an enduring one, and it is no accident that one of the most popular dog-names, Fido, is close to the Latin word for 'faith' (*fides*). Dogs were also tokens of marital fidelity. As such, they were often included on medieval tombs, lying at the feet of female effigies.

The canine link with watchfulness stems from the

traditional role of the guard-dog. In the Middle Ages, this could often have religious overtones. The authors of many bestiaries drew comparisons between a priest and a watchdog, chasing away the devil. This analogy was strengthened by the fact that cats were sometimes used as symbols of heresy. As a result, sculptors occasionally portrayed a dog biting a cat's tail, as a playful detail in church architecture.

In the Congo region of Africa, tribesmen used a *kozo* – a two-headed dog – in their rituals. Dogs were believed to have a particular significance, as mediators between the lands of the living and the dead. The *kozo* was usually represented in the form of a sacred figurine (*nkisi*). Potent medicines, covered in resin or clay, were packed into a cavity in the animal's back. Its power could then be activated by the ritual specialist (*nganga*), who would insert an iron blade into the carving, while uttering the appropriate invocations. If all went well, this power was meant to solve personal problems or bring wealth.

In many cultures there are folk tales, which feature humans who can transform themselves into dogs. In a fairy-tale from the Caribbean, for example, a young sorceress fell in love with a handsome huntsman. He seemed impervious to her charms, however, so she disguised herself as one of his hounds by casting a magi-cal dog-pelt over her shoulders. Next day, on his return from the chase, the hunter was astonished to find that his home had been swept, fresh bread had been baked, and a new fire was burning in the hearth. The same thing happened on the following day. On the third, the hunter laid a trap. He went out as normal with his dogs, but tied them to a tree and returned home early. Through the door, he saw a beautiful maiden lighting his fire, while her dog-skin lay on a chair. Immediately, he rushed in, threw the dog-skin into the fire, and claimed the woman as his bride.

Dogs were not always viewed in a positive light. In many parts of Europe, there were superstitions about a supernatural black dog, a spectral creature that haunted lonely roads and desolate moors, preying on unwary travellers. This was a creature of ill omen, that left no footprints and uttered an unearthly howling sound. If seen, it was a sign of imminent death. In many areas, there were local variants on this theme. In London's Newgate prison, a black dog was said to stalk the jail-yard on the eve of an execution. It also rode beside the driver in the cart, when the condemned man was taken off to the gallows. In Germany and Scandinavia, the devil was said to assume the form of a huge, black Poodle, with fiery eyes, glowing like red-hot coals. Mephistopheles took this guise in Goethe's *Faust*. The link between dogs and demons may stem from a passage in the Apocrypha, which suggested that Judas Iscariot was possessed. After his betrayal of Christ, the demon left him and entered the body of a dog.

With eye upraised, his master's looks to scan,
The joy, the solace, and the aid of man,
The rich man's guardian, and the poor man's friend,
The only creature faithful to the end.

George Crabbe (1755-1832)

Hunting and Sporting Dogs

The activity that forged the bond between dogs and humans was hunting. Initially, this served an obvious, practical purpose – the provision of food. Once other sources of food were available, it continued as a sport, enjoyed by the rich and powerful. The ancient Egyptians, Persians, Assyrians, and Greeks all used to hunt with dogs.

In prehistoric art, dogs were often portrayed in a highly stylised fashion, which makes them hard to identify. By the third millennium BC, this situation had changed. In Egypt, dogs resembling Greyhounds and Mastiffs were portrayed in tomb decoration and on stelae (stone slabs). Mastiffs can also be found on carved reliefs, surviving from the palace of the Assyrian king, Ashurbanipal (reigned 669-630 BC), at Nineveh. These show the dogs being used in royal hunts against lions and wild asses.

Sighthounds

Dogs detect their prey in two different ways, either by sight or by scent. Logically enough, the most common generic terms for these dogs are sighthounds and scenthounds. Sighthounds have the longer pedigree and can be traced back to at least 5,000 BC. They were also occasionally described as gazehounds, windhounds, or Greyhounds (originally a collective term). Since they always have to keep their quarry in view, the qualities of speed, agility and stamina can be found in most breeds of sighthound.

Greyhounds are certainly one of the most ancient breeds of dog. At graves in Eridu, in southern Mesopotamia, archaeologists have discovered skeletons of Greyhounds dating back to 5,000 BC. The ancient Egyptians used them to hunt gazelles, jackals, and hares, following behind the dogs in their chariots. It is possible, too, that the ambiguous form of Seth, the Egyptian god of the desert, was based on a Greyhound, although it is not the only contender. The Greeks and Romans also admired the animal, and it became the favourite hunting dog of early British rulers. Today, Greyhounds are best known as racing dogs, although their reputation in hunting circles has never declined. In the mid-19th century, they were specifically imported into the US, to help deal with a massive upsurge in the jack-rabbit population. The dog's name, incidentally, probably has nothing to do with its colour. It is more likely to be a corruption of either Greek (*Graius*) or Great Hound

In Britain, hunting with Greyhounds was reserved for members of the nobility and the royal family. This stemmed from a statute passed in 1016 by King Canute (ruled 1016-35), decreeing that 'no meane person [serf] may keep any greihounds'. Even a freeman was obliged

to have his Greyhound lamed if he lived too close to a royal forest. The associations with class and good breeding remained true in Shakespeare's time, as this extract from *Henry V* illustrates:

> 'Let us swear that you are worth your breeding;
> Which I doubt not;
> For there is none of you so mean and base,
> That hath not noble lustre in your eyes.
> I see you stand like Greyhounds in the slips,
> Straining upon the start...'

Greyhounds are not the only ancient sighthounds; Salukis and Afghans also have an extremely long pedigree. The Saluki or Gazelle Hound has been identified on Sumerian carvings and Egyptian murals. It is also possible that Tutankhamun owned dogs of this kind. If folklore is to believed, then Afghan Hounds are even older, as there is a legend that these were the dogs taken into Noah's Ark. The exotic appearance of the Pharaoh Hound may suggest that it belongs in the same company, but it was actually bred in Malta for hunting rabbits. Its present name only dates back to the 1960s, though the dog itself bears an uncanny resemblance to some of those portrayed in Egyptian tombs.

Not all sighthounds were developed in the Middle East. One of the most famous breeds, the Borzoi emerged in Russia, where it became the favourite dog of the Tsars. Its origins are disputed, but the likeliest explanation is that imported Greyhounds were combined with local, long-haired sheepdogs, to produce an animal with a thick enough coat to withstand the Russian winters. Borzois are notable for their speed (the name means 'swift') and, from the outset, their prime purpose was to hunt wolves. This was partly a matter of pest control, as wolves were a genuine menace to livestock in the northern forest areas, though the Tsars also turned it into a royal sport. Essentially, it became a form of coursing: a wolf was flushed from its hiding place and then a brace of Borzois were released to chase after it, pinning it down on either side. These events became highly ceremonial affairs, with hunters in special costumes and celebratory banquets.

In addition, the Tsars would often present pairs of Borzois to their royal relatives and other, foreign dignitaries. This was fortunate since, like the German Shepherd, the dogs were to suffer from guilt by association. To supporters of the Russian Revolution (1917), Borzois symbolised the hated Tsarist regime and thousands of them were slaughtered. The breed virtually disappeared in its native land, and later had to be reintroduced from other parts of Europe.

The Lurcher is something of an anomaly in the sighthound group. It is not a recognised breed, as its parentage can vary considerably. Usually, it is a cross between a Greyhound or a Whippet and some form of sheepdog, such as a Rough Collie or a Border Collie. Lurchers have been common since the 18th century, when the Earl of Orford used them in his breeding experiments. The dogs are highly popular, although they used to have a somewhat raffish reputation, largely because they were closely associated with poachers, gypsies and travellers. Thomas Bewick (1755-1828), the animal artist, referred to their habits as 'dark and cunning', and the name itself comes from the Romany word for 'thief' (*lur*). They evoked a more positive reaction in the verses of Patrick Chalmers (1875-1942), who admired their quiet air of intelligence:

> ... a long lean dog
> At a sling jig-jog
> A poacher to his eyelids as all the lurcher clan...

SENSE OF SMELL

The average human has 5 million scent receptors
The average Dachshund has 125 million
The average Fox Terrier has 150 million
The average German Shepherd has 200 million

SCENTHOUNDS

Sighthounds flourished in wide open spaces, such as deserts and plains. In the West, where hunting often took place in forests or other, rough terrain, scenthounds were generally preferred. Over the centuries, breeders gradually developed dogs that could carry out a range of highly specialised tasks, but initially hunters had to rely on all-round performers. In medieval sources, two names crop up frequently - St. Hubert's Hound and the Talbot Hound. In its day, the former had the finest scenting ability of any dog, but it was eventually superseded by other, swifter breeds. The Talbot Hound was one of its descendants. It had a pure white coat, but was otherwise very similar to the Bloodhound. Talbots were extremely popular throughout the Middle Ages, but gradually died out as other breeds came to the fore.

The Bloodhound is closely related to both the St. Hubert's Hound and the Talbot Hound. Initially, it was used for hunting deer and was valued, in particular, for its skill in tracking wounded animals. It was not the blood of its quarry, however, that gave the dog its name; rather, the dog itself was deemed to be of noble or pedigree blood, because it was so admired by royalty and the nobility. The Southern Hound had similar talents and, for many years, was as popular as the Bloodhound. Both dogs fell out of favour, however, when hunting trends changed. As fox-hunting replaced stag-hunting, they were found to be too slow. As a result, the Bloodhound's tracking ability was diverted to other fields, such as police work, while the Southern Hound became extinct.

Dogs were employed in hunting a wide variety of game. Often, their original quarry is obvious from their name – as in Staghound, Elkhound, Otterhound, Deerhound, and Wolfhound. Occasionally, their function is a little less clear. The Dachshund, for instance, was bred for hunting badgers (*dachs* is German for 'badger'). Similarly, the Cocker Spaniel takes its name from the birds that were its main quarry – namely the woodcock, the heathcock (black grouse), and the moorcock (red grouse).

In Britain, as in many other parts of Europe, hunting developed as a sport for a privileged elite. Only the uppermost levels of society had access to the royal forests and parks and were allowed to own the best hunting dogs. As some areas of privilege were eroded, however, the nature of hunting changed. The forests dwindled, the great estates were broken up, land was enclosed, and larger types of game – boars, stags, wolves – became less available. As a result, huntsmen were obliged to turn their attention to smaller quarry, such as foxes, hares, and birds.

There had never been an embargo on hunting these kinds of animal (foxes, for example, had long been classed as vermin), so a broader section of society became involved in the sport, with country squires and farmers joining the chase.

During the 18th century, fox-hunting replaced stag-hunting as the principal country sport. Increasingly, packs of Foxhounds and Beagles became the most popular hunting dogs. There was nothing new about hunting with packs. The ancient Greeks had done so, though they used a different method: the pack were kept on a leash, while a single hound – the Limer or Limehound – tracked down the quarry. This breed was often mentioned in medieval literature, but had become extinct by the end of the 18th century.

Hunters were keen to accentuate the primitive pack mentality of their hounds. Accordingly, they were kept together in outdoor kennels and were never treated as household pets. By contrast, other hunting breeds, such as Spaniels, Retrievers and Setters, enjoyed a much closer relationship with their masters.

As hunters switched to smaller game, they made use of a broader range of dog breeds, each of which had developed highly specialised skills. Terriers, for example, were adept at rooting out animals that had gone to ground. This is reflected in their name, which comes from *terre*, the French word for 'earth'. Equally, some dogs were proficient at flushing out birds from trees or thickets; at detecting game, but not flushing it out; or at retrieving dead or wounded creatures. Here, again, the name of the breed often provides a clue to the skill. The Pointer, for instance, adopts a distinctive 'pointing' posture once it has detected its prey. The head and neck are stretched forward, the tail is held stiffly horizontal, and a front paw is lifted, as if frozen in mid-step. The dog remains immobile in this position, indicating the location of the quarry. Setters perform a similar function, but in their case they remain 'set' in a sitting position.

'The dog that is idle barks at his fleas, but he that is hunting feels them not.'
Chinese proverb

Some of the newer hunting breeds were developed for non-sporting reasons. The West Highland White Terrier, for example, owes its origins to an unfortunate accident. While out hunting one day, Colonel Malcolm of Poltalloch mistook his favourite terrier for a fox and shot it. Vowing never to repeat this awful blunder, he decided to create a new, white terrier. He achieved this by selective breeding, using white puppies from the litters of Cairn Terriers.

Many of the breeds that were developed for hunting are now more familiar as show-dogs or pets. The Poodle, for example, was originally bred as a retriever or water dog. This is emphasised by its name, which comes from the

German word *puddeln* ('to splash in water'). The Poodle's distinctive coiffure is a legacy from these early days, rather than the show-ring. The hair was clipped short in some areas to allow the dog to move quickly through the water but was left longer around the joints and the tail to protect these in the animal's damp and chilly working conditions.

A Poodle once towed me along,
But always we came to one harbour;
To keep his curls smart,
And shave his hind part,
He constantly called on a barber.

Thomas Hood (1799-1845)

Coursing for hares is an old country pastime, which developed as an offshoot of hunting. The Duke of Norfolk drew up the earliest set of rules for the sport in Tudor times and, in the 18th century, private coursing clubs began to appear. The first one open to the public was founded in 1776 by Lord Orford. He tried to improve the performance of his Greyhounds through an extensive series of cross-breeding experiments. The latter involved Lurchers, Deerhounds and, more surprisingly, Bulldogs. Indeed, his champion courser, Czarina, was said to have some Bulldog in her veins.

Supporters of coursing argue that the aim of the sport is to test the speed and agility of competing Greyhounds, rather than to achieve a kill. At a typical meeting, the dogs are 'slipped' (released) in pairs. They gain points for their speed in catching up with the hare, for forcing it to make a turn, and for tripping or killing it. The points are awarded by a judge, who follows the action on horse-back.

The most famous trophy in the coursing world is the Waterloo Cup, which was founded in 1836 by William Lynn, a Liverpool hotelier (better known, perhaps, as the creator of the Grand National). Lynn named the cup after his establishment, the Waterloo Hotel. The first event was staged on Lord Sefton's estate at Altcar. In its heyday – around the start of the 20th century – the competition attracted huge crowds, but its popularity began to wane after the introduction of greyhound racing. It has also been targeted increasingly by protesters. Following the disruptive scenes at the 1988 competition, for example, it was dubbed 'the Battle of Waterloo' by the press. In the light of recent legislation against blood sports, some journalists have questioned whether the event can survive.

One of the best known coursing greyhounds was Master M'Grath, an Irish dog who won the Waterloo Cup three times (1868, 1869, and 1871). In his day, he was so famous that his owner, Lord Lurgan, was asked to show him to Queen Victoria. Poems were composed in his honour; a pub and a brand of pet food were named after him; and a monument was erected near his birthplace in Colligan, Co. Waterford. When he won the Waterloo Cup for the third time, crowds thronged the streets of

Dublin in celebration. The dog's mysterious death in 1871 added to his legendary status. There were rumours that he had been poisoned, and his burial place was kept secret.

Greyhound racing grew out of coursing, when some enthusiasts began to search for a humane alternative to the blood sport. One early attempt took place at Hendon, to the north of London. In September 1876, six greyhounds raced over a straight, 400-yard course, chasing a dummy hare on 'an apparatus like a skate on wheels'. The event was dubbed 'coursing by proxy', but it attracted little interest and the venture proved a failure.

The idea met with greater success in the United States. There, the pioneer was Owen Patrick Smith, a director of the Chamber of Commerce in Hot Springs, South Dakota. He replaced the straight track with an oval one and looked for ways of improving the artificial lure. His first version was a stuffed rabbit-skin, dragged behind a motorcycle. The latter was subsequently replaced by a motorised cart, travelling along a rail beside the track. This suffered from teething problems, however, as the cart occasionally came off the track, causing the cancellation of the race. By the early 1920s, these difficulties had been ironed out and Smith enjoyed considerable success with his tracks at Tulsa, Oklahoma, and East St. Louis, Illinois. The popularity of the sport really took off in 1925, however, when Smith introduced night racing, to counter complaints that his events were creating absenteeism at local firms.

The popularity of greyhound racing in the US prompted an American entrepreneur, Charles Munn, to bring the sport to Britain. In 1925, he reached an agreement with Smith over the right to use his artificial hare. Then, with the backing of several English businessmen, he launched the Greyhound Racing Association in 1926. The first race took place in July 1926 at Belle Vue, Manchester, and was won by a dog called Mistley. The event was a notable success and, in its inaugural season, a further 36 meetings were held on the same track. By 1928, the sport had become firmly established throughout the UK, with 68 stadiums either planned or in operation.

Mick the Miller became the first superstar of the sport, creating a sensation in the 1920s. He was born in an Irish vicarage, in a litter of 12 pups, and was named after Mick Miller, the handyman who helped to raise the dogs. Initially, his chances of racing seemed very poor, as he went down with distemper. Fortunately, he recovered and made his competitive debut in Ireland in 1928. Soon he was breaking record after record, and his owners decided to take him to England. There, he won the Derby in 1929 and 1930, and was sold for 2,000 guineas – a colossal sum in those days.

After retiring, Mick went on to grace the silver screen, appearing in *Wild Boy* (1934), where he foiled a gang's attempt to prevent him from racing in the Derby. The film starred Flanagan and Allen, but was not a great success at the box office. Mick's fame lived on after his death and, for many years, his embalmed body was on view at the Natural History Museum.

Greyhounds are not the only racers in the dog world. For many years, Whippet racing has also been popular. In Victorian Britain, the pastime was traditionally associated with poorer, mining areas, where the Whippet was regarded as a cheap alternative to its larger cousin (they are thought to have been bred by crossing small Greyhounds with Terriers). Whippets are faster in the sprint than Greyhounds, but they have less stamina and would fare less well on a full-length racing track. The sport developed as a form of coursing, with Whippets chasing rabbits in an enclosure. When this was condemned as cruel, it was replaced with 'rag-racing', where the dogs were set to chase a rag or cloth down a track. Instead of using traps, the dogs were released by a handler or 'slipper', who held the Whippet by the tail and neck, until the starting gun was fired. Today, Whippet racing has moved on from its working-class origins and is enjoyed worldwide, usually on an amateur basis. There are racing clubs in the United States, Australia and Finland.

Some dog races provide a test of stamina and endurance, rather than speed. This is certainly the case with the gruelling, long-distance sled-races that take place in some of the world's most forbidding conditions. In Alaska, Canada, Scandinavia, and Siberia, sled-racing or mushing is a fast-growing sport. These contests can take place over a variety of distances, ranging from a sprint race (4-25 miles), a mid-distance race (25-200 miles) or the real endurance tests, where the course is over a thousand miles long and takes several days to complete. Currently, there are moves to turn sled-racing into an Olympic sport.

The pioneering event in this field was the All Alaska
Sweepstakes, which was launched in 1908 and staged
until 1918, when the race was halted by American
involvement in World War One. The initial times were
not particularly fast, largely because the runners were
ordinary freight dogs. In 1909, however, Siberian
Huskies were introduced by a Russian fur trader, William
Goosak. These dogs were smaller than other draught
animals – unimpressed locals dubbed them 'Siberian rats'
– but they soon proved to be the fastest of all the sled
dogs. Using this breed, a driver called 'Iron Man' Johnson
won the 1910 race, setting a record time that has never
been beaten. The Husky's name, incidentally, probably
stems from a Siberian tribe, the Chukchi.

Today, the most famous sled-race takes place along the
Iditarod Trail. This historic pathway had been a vital link
during the Alaskan Gold Rush of the early 1900s, but had
largely fallen into disuse. Iditarod itself had become a
ghost town. Then in 1967, a short race (25 miles) was
proposed, to mark the centenary of the purchase of
Alaska from Russia. This aroused sufficient interest to
create a long-distance race (almost 1,050 miles) between
Anchorage and Nome. The first race was held in 1973,
and the competition has since gone from strength to
strength, attracting competitors from as far away as
Britain, Italy, France, Australia, and Japan. The record time
of 8 days, 22 hours, and 46 minutes was set in 2002.

A dog teaches a boy fidelity, perseverance,
and to turn around three times before lying down.
Robert Benchley

BREEDS &
DOG SHOWS

Dog shows began to appear in the 1830s, just as moves were made to ban the more brutal forms of canine entertainment - namely, bull-baiting and dog fights. The early events were fairly chaotic, as no breed standards had yet been set and the judging criteria varied from one contest to the next. The first organised show was staged in 1859, at the Town Hall in Newcastle-upon-Tyne.

The need for consistency in dog competitions led to the creation of clubs and societies devoted to individual breeds. They laid down the 'breed standards' – the physical qualities that marked out the ideal specimen of the breed in question. Once these standards became generally accepted, the judging at dog shows became far more reliable. One of the prime functions of the Kennel Club, which was founded in 1873, was to register the breed standards and ensure that they were adopted at all major dog competitions.

The world's most famous dog show was founded in 1891 by Charles Cruft (1852-1938). The son of a jeweller, he began his career as a travelling salesman for James Spratt's dog biscuit company, making contacts throughout the dog world. He soon recognised that there was a growing demand for dog contests and, in 1878, he organised his first show, at the World Fair in Paris. This was followed by a series of events devoted to terriers, which proved successful enough to earn him the nickname of 'the British Barnum'. Cruft's 1891 show, however, broke new ground. It was the first to be open to all breeds and the first to bear his name in the title. Cruft also achieved a massive publicity coup by persuading Queen Victoria to enter several of her dogs in the event – the first time that she had participated directly in a competition of this kind.

Spelling: It was Cruft's until 1974, when it was changed to Crufts.

BEST IN SHOW AT CRUFTS, 1928-2005

Cocker Spaniel	7 winners
Irish Setter	4
Welsh Terrier	4
English Setter	3
German Shepherd/Alsatian	3
Greyhound	3
Labrador Retriever	3
Standard Poodle	3
Wire Fox Terrier	3
Afghan Hound	2
Airedale Terrier	2
Kerry Blue Terrier	2
Lakeland Terrier	2
Pointer	2
Toy Poodle	2
West Highland White Terrier	2
Whippet	2

The 'Best in Show' title was first awarded in 1928. Prior to 1906, there was no overall prize. Between 1906 and 1928, a Challenge Bowl was sometimes awarded to the 'Best Champion in the Show'.

Not all dog shows are aimed at pedigree dogs. The Kennel Club runs a competition called Scruffts, which is open to dogs of mixed stock. Entrants compete in four different categories: the Most Handsome Crossbreed Dog, the Prettiest Crossbreed Bitch, the Child's Best Friend, and the Golden Oldie Crossbreed. Qualifying heats are held at a number of regional dog contests, and the finalists compete at the annual Discover Dogs show.

The Westminster Dog of the Year is another light-hearted dog competition, organised by the Kennel Club and the Dogs Trust. Contested by Parliamentary dog owners, the event is currently in its fourteenth year. It is open to both pedigree and crossbreed animals. In 2005, the winner was Torres, an 18-month-old Pug belonging to Tony Baldry, the Conservative MP for Banbury. The competition is designed to promote the importance of responsible pet ownership.

BREED NAMES

The majority of breed names have a geographical element, indicating where the dog originated or where it was especially popular. Thus, Rottweiler refers to Rottweil (a market town in southern Germany), Briard stems from Brie (the cheese-making district in France), Spaniel comes from *Español* (Spanish), and Chihuahua is derived from the name of a Mexican state. Occasionally, the name may be misleading. The Great Dane, for instance, is widely regarded as a German dog, while in France and England the German Shepherd became known as the Alsatian (i.e. from Alsace), to protect it from anti-German sentiments during and after the two World Wars. Similarly, there is no obvious link between the Dalmatian and the region of Dalmatia in the Balkans.

Very few dogs bear the name of their original breeder. The most famous example is the Jack Russell Terrier, which was developed by the Reverend John Russell (1795–1883) – better known by his nickname, 'Parson Jack'. From an early age, his favourite pastime was hunting and, with this in mind, he took a particular interest in terriers. While still a student at Oxford, he bought an unusual bitch called Trump from a passing milkman, and she became the founder of his breed. In developing the new strain, Russell's aim was to produce a terrier that was fast enough to keep up with the hounds, but still small enough to chase a fox from its cover. The clergyman was an equally important figure in other areas of the dog world. He became a founding member of the Kennel Club, and acted as a judge in many early dog shows.

In a rather different vein, the Dobermann Pinscher owes its name to a German tax collector called Louis Dobermann (d.1894). The Pinscher was an ancient breed, but Louis wanted to produce a larger and more aggressive variety, which could protect him while he carried out his unpopular duties. Fortunately, the dog proved easy to train and, as a result, has been widely used by the police and the army. It became the mascot of the US Marines, who nicknamed it 'the devil dog', after its service in World War II. In New York, Dobermanns were used against a less dangerous enemy. In Macy's department store, they were taken on night patrols, to help flush out any shoplifters who tried to hide in the building after closing time.

By contrast, the name of the Chinook derives from an individual dog, rather than its owner. The breed was developed by Arthur Walden, an American from New Hampshire. While working in Alaska, he became fascinated with sled dogs and decided to create his own variety. On his return to New England he embarked on this project, founding the line on a dog called Chinook (literally 'Warm Winds'), who was part Husky and part Mastiff. Walden added German Shepherd and Belgian Shepherd to this mix, to produce an unusual sled dog, resembling a Golden Labrador. In 1929, Walden joined Admiral Byrd's (1888-1957) expedition to the Antarctic, where unfortunately Chinook became separated from the main party and was lost.

Sometimes, dogs may be named in honour of an individual or an organisation. The Keeshond, for example, became a national symbol for the Dutch. 'Kees' is a popular form of Cornelis, and the dog is thought to have been named after either Cornelis de Gyselaer or Cornelis de Witt – both of whom were patriotic leaders. Certainly, the dog found favour with opponents of the aristocracy, who used the Pug as their mascot.

The reason a dog has so many friends is that he wags
his tail instead of his tongue.
Anonymous

The Griffon Nivernais and associated breeds take their name from a royal official. From medieval times, French kings were particularly fond of these lively hunting dogs and placed them in the care of a court clerk, known as a *greffier*. The name stuck and, after a time, the animals were nicknamed 'greffier's dogs'. This was later corrupted to Griffon.

Many dogs owe their name to their physical characteristics. The Barbet, for example, comes from the French word *barbe* ('beard') and is one of a number of breeds that are defined by their shaggy coat. The derivation of Bichon Frisé is linked to this. Bichon is short for Barbichon (from *barbiche* or 'short beard'), while Frisé is an abbreviation of à *poil frisé* ('with curly hair'). By the 16th century, these little lapdogs were enormously popular with the French and Spanish nobility. French courtiers used to tie ribbons in their hair and dab them with perfume, giving birth to the verb *bichonner* ('to pamper'). In Germany, the name of the Schnauzer ('whiskered snout') also stems from its hirsute appearance.

The looks and qualities of the canine species will never be entirely constant, as breeders are always experimenting with new crosses. Recently, the press has noted a growing trend for 'designer mongrels'. Apparently, the fashion started after several Hollywood stars paid high prices for Puggles (a Pug + Beagle cross). The Kennel Club do not recognise these new varieties and have warned against breeding animals simply for novelty value, as they may be born with health defects. Two of the crosses have been around for a while, however, and are already fairly well established.

The Cockapoo or Cockerpoo (Cocker Spaniel + Poodle) was developed in the US in the 1960s. The aim was to produce an ideal family pet, combining the sweet nature of the Spaniel with the non-shedding coat of the Poodle. There is a Cockapoo Club of America, but the breed cannot compete in the show-ring, because its appearance has not yet become standardised. The Labradoodle (Labrador + Poodle) originated in Australia in the 1980s. It was developed for a serious purpose – to provide a different type of guide dog. The idea was to produce an animal with a non-shedding coat, which could be used by blind people who were allergic to canine hair.

One of the most beneficial consequences of the first Cruft's show was the creation of the National Canine Defence League. In a room adjoining the main event, Lady Gertrude Stock persuaded an influential group of sympathisers to lend their support to a new charitable body, which aimed to protect strays, promote veterinary care, and campaign against animal cruelty. The organisation grew rapidly and, by 1902, had achieved a membership of 1,000 supporters. In 2003, the NCDL changed its name to the Dogs Trust. It currently boasts more than 300,000 members and, in 2005, it found new homes for 10,367 dogs.

STRAY DOG SURVEY

A survey commissioned by the Dogs Trust, to
highlight the problem of abandoned dogs.

Regional Breakdown of Stray dogs
collected in 2005

Total UK	105,201	–1% since 2004
Wales	11,433	–3%
Scotland	9,842	+23%
Midlands	17,154	+ 3%
North West	13,347	– 4%
Northern Ireland	10,856	+1%
North East	7,584	–12%
London	6,882	+9%
Central Scotland	6,878	+12%
Southern	6,291	+7%
Yorkshire	5,170	+7%
East & Anglia	4,657	–9%
South West	3,872	+7%
Borders	2,390	+7%
Northern Scotland	2,158	+69%

Number of Dogs put to sleep

Total UK	7,798	–22% since 2004
Wales	341	–15%
Scotland	573	–31%

Midlands	907	+40%
North West	729	–11%
Northern Ireland	3,787	–5%
North East	525	–53%
London	168	+17%
Central Scotland	473	–36%
Southern	71	–23%
Yorkshire	200	–36%
East & Anglia	93	+9%
South West	20	+13%
Borders	83	–23%
Northern Scotland	45	+150%

FACTS ABOUT BATTERSEA DOGS & CATS HOME

On average, there are around 400 dogs and 100 cats at the Home, but this can rise to 500 dogs and 150 cats at busy times.

Battersea receives an average of 22 dogs every day.

Over 3 million animals have been given refuge in the Home, since its foundation in 1860.

The average length of stay for a dog is 24 days.

It costs over £900 to care for each dog, irrespective of the length of its stay.

'The more I see of men, the more I like dogs'
Madame de Stael

With the rise in pet ownership came a growing concern for animal welfare. The pioneer in this field was Mary Tealby (1801-65), who founded the celebrated Dogs' Home at Battersea. In 1860, she set up the first shelter – the 'Temporary Home for Lost and Starving Dogs' – in a stable-yard in Holloway. The Home moved to its present site in 1871. Tealby's ghost is said to haunt the place, welcoming the new arrivals.

In 2004, Battersea found new homes for more than 3,600 dogs.

In the same year, it cared for over 8,600 dogs and 2,500 cats.

In an average year, Battersea drivers travel around 120,000 miles collecting strays.

In 2005, the centre changed its name to Battersea Dogs & Cats Home.

The largest influx of strays occurred in 1886, when 35,064 dogs were admitted.

The kennels use over 1,000 blankets every day.

Along with Tealby, the other great champion of canine welfare was Maria Dickin (1870-1951). In 1917, she opened the People's Dispensary for Sick Animals in a cellar in Whitechapel, in London's East End. The sign outside the clinic read: 'Bring your sick animals – Do not let them suffer – All animals treated - All treatment free'. Wishing to extend this service beyond London, Dickin embarked on a nationwide tour in 1923, travelling with a vet in a converted gipsy caravan. In 1934 she launched a new initiative, founding the Busy Bees club, to teach youngsters a greater sense of respect for animals. Its most celebrated president was the children's author, Enid Blyton (1897-1968).

In 1943, at the height of World War Two, Maria Dickin created a new award, the Dickin Medal, which rapidly gained acceptance as the animal equivalent of the Victoria Cross. By 1950, 18 dogs had become recipients of the award, mostly for their contribution to the war effort. The sacrifice of Gander, the mascot of the Royal Rifles of Canada, provides a typical example. In 1941, during the defence of Hong Kong, this huge Newfoundland saved a group of wounded soldiers by carrying away a live grenade in his mouth, losing his own life in the process.

More recently, two guide dogs – Salty and Roselle – were presented with Dickin Medals near Ground Zero in New York, for staying to help their owners during the terrorist attacks on the Twin Towers. A third medal was awarded, as a symbolic gesture, to one of the 300 Search and Rescue dogs involved in locating survivors amongst the debris.

In the UK, pet ownership has fluctuated considerably over the years. Figures produced by the Pet Food Manufacturers' Association show that the number of pet dogs reached a peak in the late 1980s, but has gradually declined since then. This is thought to be due to the growing number of households that are empty during the day – either because both partners are out at work, or because more people are living alone. By contrast, the number of cats has continued to rise, apparently because they require less maintenance. Budgerigars – the third most popular pet - have gradually fallen out of fashion. According to the PFMA, there were 3.3 million in 1965, but just 0.75 million today.

YEAR	NUMBER OF DOGS	NUMBER OF CATS
1965	4.7 million	4.1 million
1975	5.7 "	4.5 "
1980	5.6 "	4.9 "
1985	6.3 "	6.1 "
1990	7.4 "	6.8 "
1995	6.6 "	7.2 "
2000	6.5 "	8.0 "
2002	6.1 "	7.5 "

WORKING DOGS

From a very early stage, the ancient Romans used dogs to safeguard themselves and their property. Proof of this can be found at the House of the Poet in Pompeii, where a mosaic has survived, showing a ferocious watch-dog attached to a chain. Below it, the legend reads: *Cave Canem* – 'Beware of the Dog'.

In Britain, the most popular breeds of guard dog were the Mastiff and the Bandog. The latter gained its name because it was so ferocious that it had to be secured with a 'band' or chain to prevent it from indiscriminately attacking any stranger. It was lighter than the Mastiff, but more vigilant and hostile. In his catalogue of dogs, Dr. Caius described it as ideal for deterring 'theefes, robbers, spoylers, and night wanderers'. In spite of these virtues, the Bandog became extinct in the 19th century.

Not all guard dogs were charged with looking after the home. Dalmatians, for example, were mainly used as coach dogs in the UK. In the days before motorised transport, they used to run alongside their owners' carriage, when they went out riding. Their principal duty was to protect them from any footpads or ruffians that might be lurking on lonely roads, although the elegant appearance of the creatures was in itself an undoubted asset to any fashionable household. Dalmatian puppies, incidentally, are born white – their trademark spots only appear after a few weeks.

After hunting, the most common activity for dogs has been herding sheep and other forms of livestock. Initially, the main emphasis was on guarding these animals from wolves, thieves, and other predators. This explains why some of the breeds associated with sheep-herding are more notable for their size and strength, than their speed. As the need for this type of protection declined, a more nimble and agile dog was preferred. Here, the hard-working and hyperactive Border Collie proved the ideal choice. It probably took its name from the colley, a Highland sheep with black markings.

By the 20th century, flocks were increasingly left to graze on enclosed land, so the need for working sheepdogs began to dwindle. Fortunately, the growing popularity of sheepdog trials provided another outlet for their skills. Crowds were mesmerised by the spectacle of a single Border Collie controlling a wayward flock, aided only by the whistled commands of his shepherd. The trials date back to 1873, with the oldest events taking place at Bala in Wales and Longshaw in Derbyshire. The first trials were informal affairs – the winner of an early competition at Longshaw arrived at the local station in a basket marked 'Eggs – With Care' – but they soon became highly professional. The national profile of sheepdog trials was raised enormously by the success of the long-running television show *One Man and his Dog*, which was first broadcast in 1976.

Dogs have been involved in police work for many centuries although, prior to the 20th century, this was not carried out on an organised basis. From the Middle Ages, Bloodhounds were frequently used as trackers, hunting down fugitives, outlaws and poachers. The loose folds of skin on their head enables them to keep large pockets of air in contact with the olfactory nerves, giving them their unique scenting ability. Because of their tracking skills, Bloodhounds were also known as Slot Hounds (from the Old Norse *sloth*, meaning 'track'). This was corrupted to Sleuth Hound, which in turn gave rise to the use of 'sleuth' as a term for a detective.

In America, Bloodhounds became notorious through their widespread use in the pursuit of runaway slaves and escaped convicts. They have continued to play a large part in police work up to the present day. In Kentucky, one particular Bloodhound – dubbed 'Nick Carter' by his handlers – was deemed responsible for more than 600 arrests. Similarly, when James Earl Ray (the killer of Martin Luther King) broke out of jail in 1977, it was a pack of Bloodhounds that tracked him down in the Tennessee hills. In Britain, the picture is a little more mixed. Bloodhounds were instrumental in the capture of the Duke of Monmouth (1649-85), after his failed uprising against Charles II, but they proved wholly ineffective when employed in the hunt for Jack the Ripper.

In the UK, members of the Watch sometimes took a dog with them while they were carrying out their duties, and in the 1890s the officers at Hyde Park police station kept a Fox Terrier called Topper. He was untrained, however, and appears to have been used mainly for publicity purposes. The breakthrough came in Prussia, where Inspector Franz Laufer suggested using dogs on night patrols. The authorities were sceptical, but in 1900 they gave him the funding to buy three Great Danes. When one of these – a dog called Caesar – helped to track down a dangerous criminal, Laufer's superiors were convinced.

Similar trials were carried out in Belgium, using Sheepdogs, and it was the success of these that prompted the UK to experiment with the idea. In 1908, the first official police dogs – four Airedale Terriers – were deployed on patrols at Hull docks. The results were promising enough to extend the scheme to other docks and railways, but dogs were not used in street patrols until 1938, when two Labradors were employed in parts of South London.

The first dedicated training section was set up in 1953 and, today, all the UK forces have their own Police Dog Unit. Approximately 2,500 dogs are currently in service. German Shepherds are used for general duties, while Labradors or Springer Spaniels are preferred for most of the specialised tasks. These cover an ever-widening range of skills. Sniffer dogs have been used for finding drugs since 1973, and they have since been trained to detect both explosives and accelerants (as used in arson). To operate effectively, the dogs must have a close bond with their handlers. They are placed with the selected officer as puppies but, from the outset, they are treated as working dogs, rather than pets. The basic training course lasts 14 weeks. During this time, the dog is taught obedience, agility, tracking, retrieval and, when necessary, how to chase and apprehend a suspect.

The rapid rise of canine involvement in police work is evident from the experience of the New Zealand Dog Section. Founded in 1956, the dogs were called out just 55 times in 1958. By 1968, this figure had risen to 1,645. In 1999, however, police dogs attended a staggering 37,790 incidents, while the specialist animals were used on 3,403 occasions. As a result of these activities, 6,396 offenders were taken into custody, illegal substances were seized in 765 raids, and valuables amounting to more than $500,000 were recovered.

Dogs have been assisting the blind since antiquity. Confirmation of this can be found in a Roman mural at Herculaneum and in several medieval pictures. In the 18th century, a Parisian hospital for the blind tried to train dogs to help their patients, but the earliest attempts to produce an organised guide-dog system date from World War One, when thousands of soldiers were blinded by mustard gas. In 1916, a German physician named Gerhard Stalling sought to address this problem by establishing a guide-dog school in Oldenburg. This proved so successful that further training centres were created in other German cities. Soon, Stalling's efforts were producing almost 600 guide dogs a year.

After the war, the idea was taken up by a wealthy American, Dorothy Eustis. In 1928, she set up her own organisation in Switzerland and the US, which became known as *L'Oeil qui Voit* ('The Seeing Eye'). This in turn provided the inspiration for the earliest British initiative. In 1931, the first English guide dogs – four German Shepherds called Flash, Judy, Folly, and Meta – were trained in a lock-up garage in Wallasey. The Guide Dogs for the Blind Association was founded three years later and, in 1940, its first official training centre was opened in Leamington Spa.

It seems appalling today to think of dogs being used as beasts of burden, but until quite recently the practice was not unusual. For centuries, dogs were seen as a cheap alternative to horses by many poorer workers. In ancient Rome, they sometimes took part in chariot-races, when the supply of larger animals had run out. More often, they were used by tradesmen or deliverymen. It has been estimated that, in 18th-century England, more than 20,000 cart-dogs were in service. By 1850, reformers managed to have these activities banned in many parts of Europe, although some countries – most notably, Belgium and Switzerland – were still using dogs to pull milk-carts in the mid-20th century. Their favourite draught dogs were the Belgian Mastiff and the Bernese Mountain Dog. In Canada, the Newfoundland provided similar services for fishermen, helping them to land their nets and deliver their wares to market.

In the frozen wastes of Canada, Alaska and Siberia, sled dogs carried out the same kind of duties during the winter months. They carried the mail, brought timber and provisions, and transported doctors, judges, and the police between individual settlements. The dogs were usually harnessed in pairs and driven in tandem, although some drivers preferred a 'fan hitch', with each dog linked directly to the sled by its own tow-line. The most common breeds were Malamutes, which were heavy and strong, and Huskies, which were lighter but faster. These dogs were mostly pure-bred, until the arrival of gold prospectors in the late 19th century. They encouraged the growth of sled-racing as a recreation and, in a bid to produce faster animals, tried cross-breeding with smaller dogs. The development of new technology – both planes and snowmobiles – also had a huge impact on the use of sleds, rendering many of the dog-teams redundant.

In old films and stories, sled-drivers used to shout 'Mush!', when they wanted to get the dogs moving. This comes from the French word *Marche!* ('Go!'). None of the drivers actually say this now (they are much more likely to call out 'Hike!' or 'Let's go!') but, ironically, the terms 'musher' and 'mushing' have become widely accepted.

Some dogs gained lasting fame through their 'work'. In the early days of the space race, Russian scientists used animals to test the safety of their machines. The most celebrated of these was Laika, the Russian dog, which became the first living creature to be sent into orbit. This Husky crossbreed was a stray taken from the streets of Moscow. She was given the name 'Laika', because this means 'barker' in Russian. In November 1957, she was

placed aboard Sputnik 2 and launched into space. The
expedition caught the imagination of the Western press,
who dubbed the dog 'Muttnik'. The space-craft orbited
the earth 2,570 times and was burned up on re-entry, in
April 1958, although Laika had perished long before this.

Laika's flight provoked mixed reactions. In Russia, the
technical achievement was fêted and the dog was com-
memorated on a series of stamps throughout the Eastern
bloc. In the West, concerns were raised about animal
cruelty. Sputnik 2 had been completed in a hurry, so that
the expedition would coincide with the fortieth anniversary of the Russian Revolution. As a result, it was known
from the outset that it would be impossible to recover
Laika safely. Outraged, the National Canine Defence
League called upon dog lovers to observe a minute's
silence for the doomed animal. The controversy lingered
on, largely because the Soviet authorities were evasive
about the precise fate of the dog. It was only in 2002 that
an official admitted that Laika had survived for just a few
hours, before succumbing to a combination of heat and
stress. In addition, the scientist Oleg Gazenko expressed
his own regret: 'The more time passes, the more I am
sorry...We should not have done it...We did not learn
enough from the mission to justify the death of that dog'.

Later canine cosmonauts were more fortunate, as they
were usually recovered safely. In August 1960, for example, the Russians sent up two dogs, Belka and Strelka, in
Sputnik 5. They suffered no ill effects from their voyage
and, indeed, Strelka later gave birth to six pups. One of
these was given as a present to President Kennedy.

Medical experts have long been aware of the therapeutic value of owning a pet. With this in mind, Lesley Scott-Ordish founded the PAT (Pets as Therapy) charity in 1983. Through this, registered volunteers can introduce their pets to people who have no access to animals. Patients in hospital and the residents of care-homes can often feel very isolated, particularly if they have previously been pet owners themselves, and the attentions of a friendly dog can often bring very real benefits, reminding them of home comforts.

Since 1983, more than 12,000 dogs have been registered with this scheme. They are mostly used in hospital wards, although PAT dogs have also been employed to good effect in drug rehabilitation centres, schools, prisons, and young offenders' institutes.

Some dogs have earned a reputation as the 'author' of journals or diaries. In Rudyard Kipling's *Thy Servant a Dog* (1930), the narrator is a dog called Boots. More recently, Millie, Barbara Bush's pet Springer Spaniel, captured the hearts of America with her anecdotes about life in the White House. These were published in the bestseller, *Millie's Book, as dictated to Barbara Bush* (1990). The proceeds went to literacy charities. In 1989, Millie had a puppy called Spot, who was given to George W. Bush. Spot holds a unique record – she is the only dog to have lived at the White House during two separate administrations. Britain, too, has produced a canine author with political connections. In 2000, Roy Hattersley MP released *Buster's Diaries: The True Story of a*

Dog and His Man. Buster, a German Shepherd cross, had hit the headlines after being charged with attacking one of the royal geese in St. James's Park. He pleaded self-defence, but was fined £75. Undismayed, he decided to tell his story in the *Diaries*, which became a bestseller.

Dogs are not our whole life,
but they make our lives whole.
Roger Caras

If you think dogs can't count,
try putting three dog biscuits in your pocket
and then give him only two of them.
Phil Pastoret

FAMOUS DOGS AND OWNERS

There are many ancient tales, which focus on the loyalty or courage of individual dogs. All too often, these stories seem a little fanciful, but there are some cases which have the ring of truth about them. In the 18th century, when archaeologists were exploring the remains of Pompeii, they came across the skeleton of a dog. Around its neck, it had a silver collar, bearing an inscription. This announced that the dog's name was Delta and that it belonged to Severinos. It also described how Delta had saved his master's life, by fighting off a wolf that had attacked them. Further evidence of the dog's courage was provided by the manner of his death. For Delta's skeleton was curled around the body of a child, in an apparent attempt to protect him from the devastation caused by the eruption of Vesuvius.

Dogs are sometimes blamed for the actions of their masters, but few have attracted the vilification that was directed against Boye, a large white Poodle belonging to Prince Rupert (1619-82). As the nephew of Charles I (ruled 1625-49), Rupert joined the Royalist cause during the Civil War (1642-9) and was made commander of the cavalry. During this time, the young man was devoted to his dog and took him everywhere. Boye would join his master at war councils with the king and would run into battle, alongside the Prince's horse. For a time, Rupert proved an able leader, winning a series of notable victories. This appalled the Puritans, who believed that witchcraft lay at the root of it. Pamphlets circulated, which described Boye as the Prince's familiar, 'a Popish profane dog, more than half a devil, a kind of spirit'.

Boye's luck ran out at Marston Moor in 1644. He perished on the battlefield, after following his master into the thick of the fighting. The Roundheads were jubilant and published a mocking poem, *A Dog's Elegy, or Rupert's Tears*:

> Sad Cavaliers, Rupert invites you all
> That doe survive, to his Dog's Funerall,
> Close mourners are the witch, Pope, and Devill,
> That much lament your late befallen evill.

The British royal family have always been fond of dogs, none more so than Charles II (reigned 1660-85). Samuel Pepys (1633-1703) noted in his *Diary* that the king's dogs had the run of Hampton Palace and accompanied him everywhere, even on state occasions. Toy Spaniels were his particular favourite and the King Charles Spaniel was named after him, though there is no reason to suppose that he actually developed the strain. Over the years, the appearance of the animal altered, with the nose becoming flatter and the skull more domed. Some enthusiasts regretted this change and wanted to revive the old look of the breed, which could still be seen on royal portraits. This goal was pursued with added vigour after 1926, when an American named Roswell Eldridge offered a financial reward to the first person who could successfully reproduce the long-nosed variety of the dog. This was swiftly achieved, and the new breed became known as the Cavalier King Charles Spaniel.

King Charles's habit of allowing his dogs to roam freely meant that they were often lost or stolen. The following extract comes from a public advertisement, issued by a disgruntled royal official: 'We must call upon you again for a black dog between a Greyhound and a Spaniel, no white about him, only a streak on his breast and his tail a little bobbed. It is his Majesty's own dog and doubtless was stolen, for the dog was not born nor bred in England and would never forsake his master…Will they never leave robbing his Majesty? Must he not keep a dog?'

Aristocratic households often maintained a sizeable collection of dogs. These were mostly used for hunting or as guard dogs. The breed of the animals was important, as it underlined social status although, as the following passage by John Aubrey (1626-97) demonstrates, a lowly mongrel might be the most prized possession of all: 'This present Earl of Pembroke has at Wilton 52 mastives [mastiffs] and 30 greyhounds, some beares and a lyon…He also had a little cur-dog, which loved him. When the Earl dyed the dog would not goe from his master's dead body, but pined away and dyed under the hearse.'

Of all the dogs arrayed in fur,
Hereunder lies the truest cur.
He knew no tricks, he never flattered:
Nor those he fawned upon bespattered.

Jonathan Swift (1667-1745)

The ancient Egyptians were not alone in choosing to be
buried near their dogs. In Britain, several owners made
elaborate preparations for the final resting place of their
pets. If local tradition is to be believed, then one of the
most touching stories comes from Swithland, in
Leicestershire. This fell into the constituency of the MP,
Sir Joseph Danvers (1686-1753), who also served as
Deputy Lieutenant for the county. He could have been
buried inside the church, but turned this idea down, as he
could not bear to be parted from his favourite dog.
Instead, he was interred in a far less prestigious spot, at the
edge of the churchyard. Uniquely, his grave was
constructed across the boundary wall, so that part of it
was in consecrated ground, while the remainder lay
outside. This enabled the politician to be placed as close
as possible to his faithful friend.

From his earliest days, Lord Byron (1788-1824) was
passionate about dogs. When Cambridge University
barred him from keeping one of his pets in college, he
brought a bear instead, as an act of defiance. The poet had
several dogs during his lifetime, but his favourite was a
huge Newfoundland called Boatswain. The creature had
rescued him as a child, when he was lost and injured, and
the pair used to go swimming together in the lake at his

Nottinghamshire home. When Boatswain died, after being bitten by a rabid dog, Byron was determined to create a special monument to his memory. In spite of his debts, he built a lavish tomb in the grounds of Newstead Abbey and composed a moving epitaph to 'one who possessed beauty without vanity, strength without insolence, courage without ferocity, and all the virtues of man without his vices...' Byron fully intended to be buried with his dog, but he died abroad, fighting in the Greek War of Independence. Ironically, his devotion to dogs may have cost him his life, for there is a theory that he succumbed to Mediterranean tick fever – a disease spread by dog ticks.

Queen Victoria (reigned 1837-1901) also developed her fondness for dogs at a very early age. A childhood portrait shows her with one of her first dogs, a terrier called Nellie, while the favourite of her teenage years was a King Charles Spaniel called Dash. When he died in 1840, Victoria commissioned a memorial, which bore the following inscription: 'Reader, if you would live beloved and die regretted, profit by the example of Dash'. In her adult life, the Queen kept a wide variety of dogs at the kennels in Windsor Castle. These included exotic breeds – she owned one of the first Tibetan Mastiffs to be seen in Britain – though her favourites were always Skye Terriers or Collies. Victoria's interest did much to raise the status of the latter, which had hitherto been regarded as a humble shepherd's dog. The Queen also took a fervent interest in animal welfare. She vigorously opposed the cruel practice of docking tails and cropping ears, and bestowed the 'royal' prefix on the RSPCA (Royal Society for the Prevention of Cruelty to Animals).

There is a small, select band of dogs, who are far more famous than their owners. Chief among these is the Skye Terrier, who has become known to the world as Greyfriars Bobby. Fittingly for a 'bobby', he belonged to a police constable in Edinburgh, named John Gray. The little dog was utterly devoted to his master and, when Gray died in 1858, Bobby refused to be parted from him. Every day, he went and sat by his grave in Greyfriars Kirkyard. He remained there constantly, only leaving the spot to go to the same coffee house that he had frequented with his master. There, the owners continued to feed him. This routine went on, year after year, until Bobby became a local celebrity, loved and cared for by the people of Edinburgh.

When Sir William Chambers (one of the creators of Chambers Dictionary) became Lord Provost of Edinburgh, he was so impressed with Bobby's loyalty that he gave him an inscribed collar, to ensure that he would not be rounded up with other unlicensed strays. Bobby eventually died in 1872 and was buried close to his master. Shortly after his death, a bronze statue was erected just outside the cemetery, in honour of the little dog. Bobby's collar and feeding bowl are now on display in the city's museum.

The story of Greyfriars Bobby has parallels in other parts of the world. In Tokyo, for example, a large Akita dog called Hachi used to meet his master at the local railway station every evening as he returned home from work. Even after his owner died in 1925, Hachi continued to make this daily pilgrimage, hoping eventually to find his master again. He kept up this sad routine for over nine years, until his own death. In recognition of the dog's devotion, officials at Shibuya Station erected a bronze statue in his honour, naming it 'Chuken Hachi-ko' ('Loyal Dog Hachi').

A similar tale of dogs and railways is linked with Fort Benton, Montana. In the summer of 1936, an itinerant shepherd fell ill there, while travelling through the area with his dog. He died a few days later and his body was taken to the station, to be sent back home to his relatives. Nobody paid much attention to Shep, his dog, but the animal watched as his master's body was loaded onto the train and then waited patiently for his return. For the next five and a half years, he maintained a loyal vigil at the depot, meeting every train that stopped there, to see if his owner was aboard. Journalists picked up on the story and Shep became a famous name, gladdening the hearts of Depression-era Americans. His tale, however, ended in tragedy. As he grew older, Shep became slightly deaf and he was run over by a passing train. Hundreds of townsfolk attended the funeral, when the dog was buried in a spot overlooking the railway. On the fiftieth anniversary of Shep's death, local officials commissioned a statue of the dog, looking wistfully out into the distance, with his front paws resting on a railway sleeper. The inscription read: 'Shep - Forever Faithful'.

General George Custer (1839-76) was a keen devotee of Greyhounds. According to one source, he liked nothing better than to take a nap on his parlour floor, 'surrounded by a sea of Greyhounds'. He kept more than 20 of the creatures and took them everywhere, even on his military campaigns. It is said that he went out coursing with his Greyhounds on the day before Little Big Horn, where he made his famous Last Stand. One fortunate soldier was charged with the task of taking them to safety, before the fatal battle began.

Few dogs have become as instantly recognisable as Nipper (1884-95). A feisty Fox Terrier cross, he acquired his name from his unfortunate habit of nipping strangers on their ankles. He was also a highly inquisitive dog, and it was this quality that caught the eye of his owner, a struggling painter called Francis Barraud. He noticed how the little dog would cock his head and look puzzled whenever the phonograph was playing. This image stayed with the artist and, three years after Nipper's death, he painted the picture that has become known as *His Master's Voice*. Barraud tried to sell it to a phonograph company, but to no avail. He had more luck, however, when he changed the machine to a gramophone and showed Nipper staring quizzically down its horn. The picture was immediately sold and later became the trademark of RCA, as well as the source of the initials of the HMV record stores. Such was its fame that it was frequently copied or parodied - Captain Scott (1868-1912) mimicked it in a photograph during his polar expedition, using a Husky in place of Nipper.

The idea of a group of dogs racing against time in order to save human lives sounds like the far-fetched plot of a Hollywood movie. This is precisely what happened in

1925, however, when the children of Nome, Alaska, came under threat from a diphtheria epidemic. It was winter, the port was icebound, the two local planes were out of action, and the nearest available serum was hundreds of miles away in Anchorage. The only solution was to send the medicine by a relay of dog-sleds. It required a super-human effort but, in just five and a half days, they completed the 674-mile journey in record time. In all, the teams consisted of 19 mushers and around 150 dogs. Their feat became known as the 'Serum Run to Nome' or 'the Great Race of Mercy'.

The run made headline news all across the US, bringing lasting fame to two dogs. The greatest plaudits went to a black Husky called Balto and his Norwegian driver, Gunnar Kaasen, because they completed the final leg of the run. Statues of Balto were erected in Anchorage and New York's Central Park, and huge crowds came to see him, when he was in Cleveland Zoo. In 1995, an animated film of his exploits was produced by Steven Spielberg's studio. Despite this, the greatest contribution was probably made by another Norwegian, Leonhard Seppala, and Togo, his Siberian Husky, since they completed the longest and most dangerous section of the journey. Named after a Japanese admiral, Togo was taken on a US tour after the run. He appeared in stadiums, department stores and Madison Square Garden, and was presented with a gold medal by the Polar explorer, Roald Amundsen. After his death, Togo's remains were preserved and displayed at the Iditarod Trail Sled-Dog Museum.

THE GREAT RACE OF MERCY, 1925

Musher – Relay Sequence
Miles covered

'Wild Bill' Shannon – Nenana to Tolovana
52 miles
Edgar Kalland – Tolovana to Manley Hot Springs
31 miles
Dan Green – Manley Hot Springs to Fish Lake
28 miles
Johnny Folger – Fish Lake to Tanana
26 miles
Sam Joseph – Tanana to Kallands
34 miles
Titus Nikolai – Kallands to Nine-Mile Cabin
24 miles
Dave Corning – Nine-Mile Cabin to Kokrines
30 miles
Harry Pitka – Kokrines to Ruby
30 miles
Bill McCarty – Ruby to Whiskey Creek
28 miles
Edgar Nollner – Whiskey Creek to Galena
24 miles

George Nollner – Galena to Bishop Mountain
18 miles
Charlie Evans – Bishop Mountain to Nulato
30 miles
Tommy Patsy – Nulato to Kaltag
36 miles
Jackscrew – Kaltag to Old Woman Shelter
40 miles
Victor Anagick – Old Woman Shelter to Unalakleet
34 miles
Myles Gonangnan – Unalakleet to Shaktoolik
40 miles
Leonhard Seppala – Shaktoolik to Golovin
91 miles
Charlie Olson – Golovin to Bluff
25 miles
Gunnar Kaasen – Bluff to Nome
53 miles

Total: 674 miles

For a few days in 1966, the most famous dog in Britain was a black-and-white mongrel called Pickles. On March 20, the Jules Rimet trophy – the prize for football's World Cup – was stolen, while on display at a stamp exhibition. Red-faced officials launched a nationwide hunt, but to no avail. The cup appeared to have vanished without trace. Then on March 27, while Pickles and his owner were out walking in the London suburb of Norwood, something caught the dog's attention. He started pawing furiously at a package, wrapped in newspaper and hidden under a bush. It turned out to be the missing trophy and Pickles was acclaimed the hero of the day. England went on to win the competition later that year, but the Jules Rimet trophy was stolen again in 1983, in Rio de Janeiro. It has never been recovered.

Just like their literary counterparts, many painters have used their talents to highlight the finer qualities of their pets. In recent years, the most impressive examples have been produced by the British artist, David Hockney. In 1993, he embarked upon a series of pictures of his Dachshunds, Stanley and Boodgie. They were shown eating, walking or sprawled luxuriantly across their favourite cushion. Hockney soon found that dogs make frustrating models, however, as they are distracted by the slightest sound. So he took to leaving sheets of paper and drawing materials scattered all around his home, ready to start sketching at a moment's notice.

DOGS AND
POPULAR CULTURE

Writers and artists have been celebrating the virtues of man's best friend since ancient times. The first example of note crops up in Homer's *Odyssey*. After playing a successful part in the Trojan War, the gods delay Odysseus' return home for many years. When he finally arrives, disguised as a beggar, none of his friends or family recognise him. The one exception is his favourite hound, Argus. In his prime, this dog had been a great hunter, but Odysseus finds him lying on a dung-heap, sick, flea-ridden and neglected. Even in his weakened state, Argus recognises his old master instantly and wags his tail. He tries to rise up from his foul bed, but the effort is too much and he sinks down dead.

From medieval times, royal and noble figures often arranged for the inclusion of their dogs in official portraits and, by the 18th century, there was a growing fashion for portraying these pets on their own, without their masters. In many country houses, these canine pictures were given the same prominence as ancestral portraits. There were fine artists working in this field: the earliest-dated painting by Thomas Gainsborough (1727-

88), for example, was a portrait of a Bull Terrier called
Bumper, 'a most remarkable sagacious cur'. Inevitably,
this type of canine memento was mainly designed for the
wealthy, but in the 19th century a cheaper alternative
emerged. During Victoria's reign, there was a taste for
sentimental or anecdotal pictures of dogs, that were
widely reproduced as prints. The most popular artist
working in this vein was Sir Edwin Landseer. He holds a
unique distinction, as the only painter to have a breed of
dog named after him – the Landseer is a variant of the
Newfoundland.

For those Victorian dog-owners who did not care for
prints, there was a ready alternative. From the 1840s,
Staffordshire potters began producing large numbers of
canine figurines. These were usually designed as facing
pairs and often had flat backs, so that they could be
displayed at either end of a mantelpiece. By far the most
popular choice of dog was a shaggy, black-and-white
Spaniel, sometimes accompanied by a child. Other breeds
were also portrayed, however, most notably Greyhounds,
Pugs, Dalmatians, and Poodles.

Early Punch and Judy shows often featured a dog called
Toby, who traditionally wore a ruff with bells around his
neck, to frighten away the devil. It is unclear whether the
character was originally a puppet or a live, performing
dog. His name was probably inspired by the faithful dog,
belonging to the Old Testament figure, Tobias (Toby is a
popular form of Tobias). His story was told in the Book
of Tobit, in the Apocrypha.

The hot dog acquired its jocular name in America in the late 19th century. In 1893, at the World Fair in Chicago, a German vendor was selling hot sausages to tourists. He provided his customers with gloves, to prevent them from burning their hands, but they kept taking these away as souvenirs. So, in a bid to save costs, he placed the sausage in a long roll. The idea caught on and, soon, this became the favourite snack at baseball games. At every match, vendors could be heard crying out: 'Dachshund sausages, red hot!' (German sausages were already known as 'Dachshunds', on account of their shape). This prompted a famous sports cartoonist, Tad Dorgan (1877-1929), to draw a humorous sketch of a Dachshund inside a bun. He sent it to his editor but, as he was unsure how to spell 'Dachshund', he simply labelled it 'Hot Dog'.

There is a well known verse about dogs, composed by Isaac Watts (1674-1748):

> Let dogs delight to bark and bite,
> For God hath made them so;
> Let bears and lions growl and fight,
> For 'tis their nature too.

In 1895, when hot dogs were still a novelty, a waggish student produced an amusing parody of this for the *Yale Record*:

> "Tis dogs' delight to bark and bite,"
> Thus does the adage run.
> But I delight to bite the dog,
> When placed inside a bun

Published in 1902, *The Hound of the Baskervilles* is arguably the most famous of the Sherlock Holmes stories, while the monstrous dog itself provided the detective with one of his most testing challenges. Sir Arthur Conan Doyle (1859-1930) seems to have based the creature on a Dartmoor legend. This related how a local squire acquired such a scandalous reputation that, when he died in the 1670s, a pack of ghostly black dogs raced across the moor, breathing fire and uttering terrifying howls.

The Russian scientist, Ivan Pavlov (1849-1936), gained lasting fame through his research into canine behaviour. Originally destined for the priesthood, he turned to science and, in 1904, won the Nobel Prize for his work on the digestive system in mammals. This led him to explore related matters, such as the secretion of saliva – a relevant area to study, as the fluid helps to make food easier to swallow. Pavlov was aware that dogs salivated when they saw food, but became intrigued when he noticed that they also drooled when there was no food present. Eventually, he realised that the stimulus came from his technician's lab coat. He normally brought the dogs their food, so the mere sight of his coat awakened a sense of anticipation in them.

Pavlov then embarked on a famous series of experiments with a bell. By ringing a bell every time food was delivered, he made the dogs associate the sound with the pleasurable experience of eating. After a while, he found that they would drool whenever they heard the bell, even if no food was brought in. Pavlov defined this as a conditioned reflex. His discoveries about conditioning have proved useful in very different fields. They have been employed in the treatment of certain phobias, but have also been exploited by advertisers, wishing to associate positive feelings with their product.

Pavlov would doubtless have been impressed by the various stunts performed by Rin Tin Tin, one of the most famous canine film stars. This celebrated German Shepherd Dog was found by an American soldier in 1918. He rescued the puppy from a bombed-out army trench in Lorraine and named it after a French puppet, which had been given to the troops by local children. Returning to the US, he trained the animal and took it to Hollywood. There, Rin Tin Tin proved a huge success, starring in 26 films between 1923 and his death in 1932. At the peak of his fame, he was receiving thousands of fan letters every week. He is said to have died in the arms of Jean Harlow.

The name did not die with the dog. In 1954, it was revived for a long-running television series, *The Adventures of Rin Tin Tin*. Set in the 1880s, this Western was screened in the US until 1959 (1956-61 in the UK).

The part of the canine hero was played by descendants of the original Rin Tin Tin. There is a Rin Tin Tin museum in Latexo, Texas.

The Belgian writer and artist, Georges Hergé (1907–83), based his entire career around the simplest of concepts – the adventures of a boy and his dog. His comic-books of Tintin and Milou (renamed Snowy in Britain) were popular for more than 50 years, winning fans around the globe. The dog, a white Fox Hound, appeared in all the stories, starting with *Tintin in the Land of the Soviets* (1929). Milou's sarcastic remarks (which, of course, Tintin cannot hear) provide much of the comedy in the books, while his curiosity and his taste for whisky land them in many scrapes. Hergé took the name of his canine hero from a contraction of Marie-Louise, his first girlfriend. In spite of this, Milou appears to be a male dog. In different parts of the world, he is also known by a variety of other names, including Bobbie (Holland), Terry (Denmark), Struppi (Germany), Tobbi (Iceland), Melok (Russia), and Boncuk (Turkey).

The most lovable of Walt Disney's many canine creations was Mickey Mouse's dog, Pluto. As a character he evolved rapidly, making his first appearance in *The Chain Gang* (1930), where Mickey played an escaped convict and he was one of the pack of Bloodhounds following his trail. Later that year, he was transformed into Minnie Mouse's dog, Rover, in *The Picnic*. It was only in *The Moose Hunt* (1931) that he acquired his celebrated name. This was undoubtedly inspired by the publicity surrounding the planet Pluto, which had been discovered in 1930 by the American astronomer, Clyde Tombaugh.

Over the years, the *Lassie* films produced the same boost in popularity for Collies that *Rin Tin Tin* had provided for German Shepherds. The original source was a novel by Eric Knight (1897-1943), based on his Yorkshire childhood and on Toots, his pet Collie. In 1943, the book was turned into a huge Hollywood hit, *Lassie Come Home*. This launched the careers of both Elizabeth Taylor and her canine co-star. His real name was Pal and, like most of the other dogs in the series, he was a laddie, rather than a lassie. Pal was groomed for stardom by Frank and Rudd Weatherwax, the brothers who had already trained Dorothy's dog, Toto, in *The Wizard of Oz*. The success of the film spawned a host of sequels and spin-offs. There were five more *Lassie* films in the 1940s, a radio show, a long-running television series (1956-75), as well as a cartoon version (*Lassie's Rescue Rangers*). The most recent film, starring Peter O'Toole, was produced in 2005.

While Lassie raised the profile of Rough Collies, the adventures of Black Bob performed a similar, if more modest service for Border Collies. The stories and comic-strips of 'Black Bob, the Dandy Wonder Dog' appeared in *The Dandy* for more than 30 years, running from 1944 to 1982.

Snoopy is the most endearing character in the *Peanuts* cartoons, created by Charles M. Schulz. He has been described as 'an extroverted Beagle with a Walter Mitty complex'. First appearing in 1950, he can walk on two legs like a human, but spends most of his time lying on top of his kennel, daydreaming and philosophising. In these fantasies, he is a golf pro, a famous author, a World War One flying ace, and the dashing Joe Cool.

With its uniquely glamorous appearance, the Dalmatian might have been made for show-business. The breed reached new heights of popularity in the 1950s, follow-ing the success of *The Hundred and One Dalmatians* (1956), a best-selling novel by Dodie Smith (1896-1990). The book was turned into one of Walt Disney's most successful animated features (*101 Dalmatians*, 1961), and has since been remade with live actors. The story revolves around a plot by the villainess, Cruella da Vil, to kidnap a huge litter of puppies, in order to steal their hides. Smith got the idea for the book, after one of her friends joked that her pet Dalmatian would make a good fur coat.

It comes as no surprise to learn that Dodie Smith herself was passionate about Dalmatians and owned a succession of them. Her first Dalmatian was called Pongo – the name she used for the hero of her novel. She was also well acquainted with the business of rearing puppies. Two of her Dalmatians, Folly and Buzz, produced no fewer than 15 pups. Smith was born in Lancashire, but lived in the US during World War Two. She delayed her return to England for several years, because she could not bear the thought of her dogs going into quarantine.

'Running dog' was a common term of abuse in Maoist China. Translated from the Mandarin *zou* ('running') *gou* ('dog'), it meant 'servile follower' and was directed against any supporter of counter-revolutionary ideas. The analogy was with dogs that mindlessly obeyed their master's orders.

The long-running series of *Fred Basset* cartoons was the brainchild of Scottish artist, Alex Graham (1917-91). After forging a reputation with his *Wee Hughie* strip, which appeared for many years in Dundee's *Weekly News*, he was invited by the *Daily Mail* to produce a humorous series about a thinking dog. Shortly afterwards, in July 1963, Fred made his debut in the paper. Graham had previously owned several different breeds of dog although, surprisingly perhaps, never a Basset Hound. The public took to the cartoons instantly, although a number of Basset owners did remark that Fred bore little resemblance to the breed. As a result, the *Daily Mail* took the unusual step of giving Graham a Basset Hound, which he duly named Freda, so that he would have a live model to work from. After this, the cartoons went from strength to strength, and were soon syndicated around the world. Sometimes, the name was changed, so that Fred became Pitko in Finland, Wurzel in Germany, and Loreng in Norway. In the 1970s, Fred also appeared in a series of five-minute cartoon films, voiced by Lionel Jeffries.

In recent years, some of the most memorable canine creations have been produced for children's television. One of the quirkiest examples was Dougal, a leading

character in *The Magic Roundabout*. Loosely based on a
Maltese Terrier, he wheeled mischievously around the
set in a never-ending quest for lumps of sugar, passing
sarcastic comments about the other members of the cast.
The stop-motion animation series originated in France
in 1963. There, the dog, called Pollux, boasted a comical
English accent. In 1965, the series came to Britain, where
it was re-voiced by Eric Thompson. He wrote new
scripts, renamed the dog Dougal, and gave him a dry
sense of humour, which he likened to that of the come-
dian, Tony Hancock (1924-68). The series lasted until
1977 in the UK, but also inspired two films: *Dougal and
the Blue Cat* (1972) and *The Magic Roundabout* (2005),
where a CGI version of Dougal was voiced by Robbie
Williams.

Some dogs have enjoyed starring roles on television, but
those appearing in adverts have arguably created a far
more lasting impact. The Dulux dog and the Andrex
puppy are such familiar terms that they are now virtually
synonymous with the breed names. The association
between the Old English Sheepdog and the Dulux ads
stretches back more than four decades. Dash was the
name of the first dog to take up the role in 1964. When
he retired, after ten years of service, more than 450
owners entered the competition to provide his replace-
ment. The winning dog – Fernville Lord Digby – was
chosen at a glitzy contest at the Café Royal.

The Andrex ads have an equally long pedigree, dating
back to 1972. Since then, the trademark Labrador puppy
has unravelled numerous toilet rolls, covered itself in

feathers, and befriended a duck, a rabbit and an elephant. The company has also carried out promotions with the National Canine Defence League and the Guide Dogs for the Blind Association.

Another long-running campaign was launched in 1967, when advertisers teamed up the Liberal MP, Clement Freud, with a Bloodhound called Henry, to create a series of lugubrious ads for Chunky dog food. These proved very popular, even though Henry was concealing a secret. The dog's real name was Sanguine Saturn and he was a she, who would later produce a litter of puppies.

Dogs have left an enduring mark on popular music. On the Beatles' *White Album*, 'Martha My Dear' was inspired by Sir Paul McCartney's Old English Sheepdog. He also got the idea for 'The Fool on the Hill' after taking Martha out for an early morning walk on Primrose Hill and, with her in mind, is supposed to have added a high-pitched sound at the end of 'A Day in the Life', which only dogs can hear. Another Old English Sheepdog was featured on the cover of his live album (1993), walking along the celebrated zebra-crossing on Abbey Road.

In a similar vein, the Bonzo Dog Doo-Dah Band took their name from a cartoon dog created by George Studdy, which was famous in 1920s. 'Hound Dog' (a slang term for a scrawny mutt) proved a huge hit for both Elvis Presley and Big Mama Thornton, while 'Hound Dog' Taylor was a raunchy blues guitarist. There was a distinctly music-hall flavour to the comic numbers

'Daddy wouldn't buy me a Bow-Wow' and 'How much is that Doggie in the Window', while going further back, Stephen Foster (1826-64) wrote one of his most successful songs about his pet Setter, 'Old Dog Tray'.

Scooby Doo, Where are You? was a long-running cartoon series, first screened in September 1969. Produced by Hanna-Barbera, it focused on a group of youngsters and a rather cowardly Great Dane, as they travelled around in a van called 'The Mystery Machine', solving a variety of supernatural mysteries. The dog was originally meant to be a minor character, but the show's creator changed his mind after listening to the Frank Sinatra hit, *Strangers in the Night*. The phrase 'scooby-dooby-doo' stuck in his mind, giving him the idea for his canine hero's name. In the cartoons, Scooby was voiced by Don Messick, who had also played Boo-Boo in *Yogi Bear* and Bamm-Bamm in *The Flintstones*.

In J.K. Rowling's *Harry Potter* books, Hagrid owns two very different dogs. Fang is a large but cowardly Boarhound. In stark contrast, Fluffy is the ferocious, three-headed hound, who guards the subterranean chamber, where the Philosopher's Stone is concealed. He is clearly based on Cerberus, the gatekeeper of Hades in Greek mythology (see p.6) and, appropriately enough, Hagrid acquired the creature from a Greek man in a pub. Like Cerberus, Fluffy can be lulled to sleep by soothing music.

One of the most unusual dog-related films of recent years was a picture from Argentina, *Bombón el Perro* (2004), which became a surprise hit on the art-house cinema circuit. This was a parable about a redundant, middle-aged man, who made the painful discovery that society placed a higher value on his prize-winning, pedigree dog than on himself. Fittingly, the real star of the show was the dog – a Dogo Argentino or Argentinian Mastiff. This striking creature was an example of a modern breed, developed over a 20-year period by two brothers and introduced in 1947. Few people in the UK will have seen one, however, since this was one of the three breeds banned under the Dangerous Dogs Act of 1991.

For today's children - not to mention, many adults – the most popular canine hero of all is the star of the *Wallace and Gromit* films. Nick Park dreamt up his hilarious duo, while still a student at art school in Sheffield. Not surprisingly, his initial ideas for the characters were very different from the finished product. Gromit, for example, was originally visualised as a cat, until Park decided that a dog would be more practical. Its chunkier form would be easier to work in clay. Similarly, his earliest sketches of the animal are almost unrecognisable: in them, Gromit resembles a glove puppet with broad, flapping ears, short, stubby paws, and tiny, hooded eyes.

Pluto may have been the classic dumb mutt, but in the adventures of Wallace and Gromit, the relationship between owner and pet is reversed. Gromit is shrewd and prudent, and can often be seen shaking his head at his master's madcap schemes. He never speaks in the finished films, although dialogue is always written for him at the storyboard stage. Gromit conveys this through his marvellously expressive eyebrows, which can register any emotion, from mild enquiry to sheer disbelief.

The *Wallace and Gromit* films are peppered with delightful puns and canine jokes. In *The Wrong Trousers*, for example, Gromit's bedroom is decorated with a bone-motif wallpaper and he is shown perusing a copy of Pluto's (Plato's) *Republic*. Similarly, in *A Close Shave*, the reading matter includes *Crime and Punishment* by Fido (Fyodor) Dostoievsky and a newspaper called the *Daily Beagle* (Bugle).

*Anybody who doesn't know what soap tastes like
never washed a dog.*
Franklin P. Jones

*If I have any beliefs about immortality, it is that certain dogs
I have known will go to heaven, and very, very few persons.*
James Thurber

If your dog is fat, you aren't getting enough exercise.
Unknown

*My dog is worried about the economy because Alpo
is up to $3.00 a can. That's almost $21.00 in dog money.*
Joe Weinstein

*Ever consider what our dogs must think of us?
I mean, here we come back from a grocery store with the
most amazing haul – chicken, pork, half a cow.
They must think we're the greatest hunters on earth!*
Anne Tyler

*Women and cats will do as they please, and men and dogs
should relax and get used to the idea.*
Robert A. Heinlein

*If you pick up a starving dog and make him prosperous,
he will not bite you; that is the principal difference
between a dog and a man.*
Mark Twain

BIBLIOGRAPHY

Dale-Green, Patricia - *Dog*, Rupert Hart-Davis Ltd., 1966

Fogle, Dr. Bruce - *RSPCA Complete Dog Care Manual*,
Dorling Kindersley, 1993

Hubbard, Clifford - *Dogs in Britain*, Macmillan & Co. Ltd., 1948

Jackson, Frank - *Crufts, The Official History*, Pelham Books, 1990

Lewis, Martyn - *Dogs in the News*, Little, Brown & Co. Ltd., 1992

Merlen, R.H.A. - *De Canibus: Dog and Hound in Antiquity*,
J.A. Allen, 1971

Mery, Fernand - *The Dog*, Editions Robert Laffont, 1968

Morris, Desmond - *Dogwatching*, Jonathan Cape Ltd., 1986

Morris, Desmond - *Dogs*, Ebury Press, 2001

Secord, William - *Dog Painting 1840-1940*,
Antique Collectors' Club, 1992

Trew, Cecil G. - *The Story of the Dog*

Troy, Suzanne - *Dogs, Pets of Pedigree*, David & Charles, 1976

Various Authors - *The National Geographic Book of Dogs*,
National Geographic Society, 1958

Watson, J.N.P. - *The World's Greatest Dog Stories*,
Century Publishing, 1985

USEFUL WEBSITES

www.the-kennel-club.org.uk - The Kennel Club & Crufts

www.pdsa.org.uk - People's Dispensary for Sick Animals

www.dogshome.org - Battersea Dogs & Cats Home

www.greyfriarsbobby.co.uk - Greyfriars Bobby
and other famous dogs

www.dogstrust.org.uk - Dogs Trust

www.thedogs.co.uk - Greyhound Racing

www.pfma.com - Pet Food Manufacturers Association

www.btp.police.uk - Police Dog Pioneers

www.rintintin.com - Rin Tin Tin

www.petplace.com - Pet Care and History

www.giga-usa.com - Dog Quotes

www.brownielocks.com/iditarod - History of the Iditarod Race

www.sheepdogchampionships.co.uk - Bala Sheepdog Trials

www.guidedogs.org.uk - Guide Dogs

Links are to home pages